# CONTENTS

INTRODUCTION...2

ALMOND AND PINE NUT COOKIES...6

CHOCOLATE ROCKY ROAD...8

LEMON BUTTER BISCUITS...10

BEAUTIFUL BLACK FOREST CUPCAKES...12

BUTTERNUT SQUASH MUFFINS WITH A FROSTY TOP...14

SEA SALT AND CARAMEL CHOCOLATE CAKE...16

CARROT AND HONEY CAKE...18

BLUEBERRY BAKEWELL TART...20

STICKY TOFFEE CUPCAKES...22

CHILDREN'S PARTY CAKE...24

CHOCOLATE BROWNIES...26

STICKY RHUBARB AND GINGER CAKE...28

HOME-MADE FUDGE...30

THANKS...32

# INTRODUCTION

WELCOME TO MY MONSTER BAKE SALE BOOK! THIS IS MY FOURTH COOKBOOK FOR RED NOSE DAY, AND I THINK IT'S THE VERY BEST YET. MY LAST RED NOSE COOKBOOK MADE £899,352 FOR CHARITY, AND OVER THE PAST THREE RED NOSE DAYS THESE LITTLE BOOKS HAVE RAISED £2,281,160 IN TOTAL. I REALLY WANT THIS ONE TO RAISE MORE MONEY THAN EVER SO PLEASE, PLEASE, GET EACH OF YOUR MATES TO BUY A BOOK. IT ONLY COSTS £3, AND OUT OF THAT £2.50 GOES DIRECTLY TO COMIC RELIEF SO THEY CAN PUT IT TO GOOD USE. THE REMAINING 50P PAYS FOR THE PRINTING AND DISTRIBUTION OF THIS LITTLE BOOK.

THIS YEAR'S BOOK IS A SPECIAL ONE FOR ME BECAUSE COMIC RELIEF IS GOING TO GIVE HALF OF THE £2.50 RAISED FROM THE BOOK TO THE JAMIE OLIVER FOUNDATION. SOME OF THE MONEY WILL HELP US KICK OFF OUR KITCHEN GARDEN PROJECT IN PRIMARY SCHOOLS AROUND THE COUNTRY. THIS IS GOING TO MAKE FOOD EDUCATION A GREAT AND MEANINGFUL THING THAT WILL EMPOWER KIDS, TEACHERS AND PARENTS TO ENJOY FOOD AND MAKE BETTER CHOICES FOR THEMSELVES AND THEIR FUTURE FAMILIES. IT'S GOING TO BE INCREDIBLE, SO BIG LOVE TO COMIC RELIEF, AND THANK YOU FOR BEING A PART OF IT BY BUYING THIS BOOK.

YOU MIGHT NOT KNOW THIS, BUT LOADS OF THE MONEY COMIC RELIEF RAISES COMES FROM PEOPLE AROUND THE UK SELLING BAKED GOODS AT THEIR SCHOOLS, OFFICES OR CLUBS. SO THIS YEAR, I'VE DECIDED TO CELEBRATE THE POWER OF THE CAKE, AND PUT THIRTEEN (THAT'S RIGHT, A BAKER'S DOZEN) OF MY TASTIEST BAKE SALE TREATS IN THIS LITTLE BOOK. THERE ARE SOME REAL GEMS IN HERE. SO, ONCE YOU AND YOUR MATES ALL HAVE YOUR OWN COPIES, DIVVY UP THE RECIPES AND GET BAKING. YOU'LL HAVE MORE THAN ENOUGH TREATS BETWEEN YOU TO HOLD YOUR OWN 'MONSTER BAKE SALE' FOR COMIC RELIEF. HAVE A LAUGH, EAT SOME LOVELY THINGS, DISCOVER SOME NEW FAVOURITE RECIPES AND RAISE MONEY FOR A FANTASTIC CAUSE.

ALL OF THE MONEY RAISED FROM THE SALE OF THIS COOKBOOK WILL GET PUT TO SUCH GOOD USE BY COMIC RELIEF. I'VE SEEN IT MYSELF AND THERE'S WORK HAPPENING BEHIND THE SCENES EVERY DAY TO MAKE SURE THAT EVERY PENNY RAISED ENDS UP HELPING SOMEBODY WHO REALLY NEEDS A STROKE OF LUCK. IT MIGHT BE HERE IN BRITAIN, IT MIGHT BE IN SOME HARD-TO-REACH PART OF THE WORLD, BUT THEY ARE HAVING THEIR LIVES IMPROVED AND BEING GIVEN FANTASTIC OPPORTUNITIES BECAUSE OF YOUR HELP. SO BIG THANKS FOR BUYING THIS BOOK. THERE'S ABSOLUTELY NO REASON FOR IT TO BE THROWN IN THE BIN ONCE RED NOSE DAY IS OVER BECAUSE EVERY SINGLE RECIPE IN HERE IS TRIED, TESTED AND GENUINELY DELICIOUS. KEEP IT WITH YOUR OTHER RED NOSE BOOKS, AND PULL IT OUT ANY TIME YOU'VE GOT SOMETHING TO CELEBRATE.

LOTS OF LOVE, AND HAPPY BAKING!

*Jamie*

# RAISE A TASTY SUM

Jamie's cakes look so mouth-wateringly delicious, we wouldn't blame you if you ate them all yourself. But, if you do fancy throwing on your pinny and rustling up a batch to sell for Red Nose Day, you'll be making a huge difference. That's because flogging yummy treats to peckish cake lovers is one simple recipe for raising loads of cash and helping to change lives.

Here are a few tips to make your monster bake sale the most successful ever:

- Sell your wares at work or school – hungry colleagues and classmates will snap them up at break time.
- Get friends to bake too – the more the merrier, and the more you'll sell. Just make sure they don't eat too much of the cake mixture.
- Hold a bake-off or a cake-decorating competition. You can all pay to enter and show off your baking skills, and you'll have lots of yummy treats to bribe the judge.

You can also find loads of other great ideas for raising cash at rednoseday.com.

If you do get baking and raise some dosh from a cake sale, it could make an even bigger difference to people's lives across Africa and the UK. Just take a look at what you could do:

- £10 could provide a week's worth of healthy dinners at a drop-in centre for a child living in poverty in the UK.
- £25 could pay for an in-depth phone call between a young UK runaway, their parents and a Helpline staff member. This is often the vital first step towards re-building a fractured relationship.
- £100 could pay for a street child living in Tanzania to attend secondary school for a whole year.

So start making, start baking and they'll sell like hot cakes!

# MAKE A CAKE AND MAKE A DIFFERENCE

When you buy this brilliant little recipe book, £2.50 will come straight to Comic Relief to help transform lives. Half the cash will be used to support the Jamie Oliver Foundation and its great work.

The remaining £1.25 will go to other amazing projects across the UK and Africa, which help people living unimaginably tough lives. It could buy enough pens and paper for five children living on the streets in Ethiopia to use at school. Getting an education is their only real chance to escape poverty and create a better future for themselves.

The Jamie Oliver Foundation is a registered charity that aims to empower and improve lives through food. The Foundation teaches, trains and employs people, and provides good, clear information about food and cooking to as many people as possible.

# ALMOND AND PINE NUT COOKIES

MAKES ABOUT 24 COOKIES

These delicious little cookies are a twist on the classic American peanut-butter cookie. They've got a toasty, crunchy outside and a gorgeous chewy centre, and are so nice when they're still a little warm from the oven.

150g unblanched whole almonds
a large handful of pine nuts
110g caster sugar
75g light soft brown sugar
100g unsalted butter
1 large egg, preferably
 free-range or organic

2 tablespoons golden syrup
1 tablespoon good-quality
 vanilla extract
150g plain flour
1 teaspoon bicarbonate of soda
35g rolled porridge oats

Preheat your oven to 180°C/350°F/gas 4. Spread the almonds and pine nuts on a roasting tray and put them into the hot oven for 5 minutes. Once they're beginning to colour slightly, take them out and save a couple of handfuls for later. Blitz the rest up in a food processor until you get coarse crumbs. Add your sugars, butter, egg, golden syrup, vanilla extract, flour and bicarbonate of soda, and pulse for a few minutes until nice and smooth.

Spoon this mixture into a large bowl and add the porridge oats. Roughly chop the reserved nuts and fold these into the mixture really well, using a wooden spoon.

Line 2 large baking sheets with baking parchment. Use a tablespoon to spoon dollops of the cookie mixture on to your trays, leaving enough space between them for the cookies to spread without touching. Resist the urge to flatten them down if they are sitting quite high on the tray.

Bake the cookies in the hot oven for 10 minutes until golden around the edges. If they're still a bit gooey in the middle when you take them out, that's all right, because they'll harden up a bit as they cool. Leave them on the tray for about 10 minutes, then carefully transfer them to a wire rack to cool for 5 minutes or so. Pop them in a cookie jar and they'll keep for a few days.

# CHOCOLATE ROCKY ROAD

## MAKES 20 CHUNKY PIECES

I remember those chocolate fridge cakes from back in the day that had meringue, porridge oats and other bits and pieces in them. This colourful treat has a similar vibe. I've used all sorts of lovely dried fruits like mango, nuts and even red chillies, which might sound a bit scary but is actually quite subtle and delicious.

400g good-quality dark chocolate (70% cocoa solids)

½–1 fresh red chilli, deseeded and finely chopped

200g mixed unsalted nuts, such as almonds, hazelnuts, pistachios or pecans

2 tablespoons sunflower or pumpkin seeds

200g mixed dried fruit, such as golden raisins, dried mango, dried sour cherries or cranberries, larger bits chopped

Preheat your oven to 200°C/400°F/gas 6. Smash up the chocolate and melt it in a heatproof glass bowl over a pan of simmering water, making sure the bowl doesn't touch the water. Once the chocolate is smooth and melted, remove the bowl from the heat and put to one side. While the chocolate is melting, put the chopped chilli pieces on a baking tray with the mixed nuts and the seeds. Place in the hot oven for 5 minutes, until the nuts are toasted and shiny. Leave to cool for a few minutes, then roughly chop everything together on a board and mix with the dried fruit in a bowl.

Put a large handful of this fruit and nut mixture to one side, and tip the rest into the bowl of chocolate. Stir well until everything is completely coated. Line a 20cm x 30cm baking tray with a piece of greaseproof paper and spoon the chocolate mixture on to it, using the back of a spoon to smooth it out to the sides. Sprinkle the reserved fruit and nuts evenly over the top, and leave in a cool place or in the fridge for 30 minutes to set.

Once the rocky road has set, break it up into bite-size chunks or larger pieces and pile up on a serving plate. Lovely with a cup of coffee, or even finely bashed up over some good-quality vanilla ice cream. Any leftover bits will keep happily for up to a week in an airtight container but you'll struggle to keep them around that long!

# LEMON BUTTER BISCUITS

MAKES ABOUT 30 BISCUITS

These biscuits are easy to make and perfect for a bake sale like this. If you want to play around with the flavours, try using an orange in place of the lemons and adding a pinch of cinnamon to your demerara – lovely!

125g butter, at room temperature
100g caster sugar
1 large egg, preferably free-range
  or organic
200g plain flour, plus extra for dusting

juice and zest of 2 lemons
¼ teaspoon baking powder
a pinch of sea salt
3 tablespoons demerara sugar

Beat the butter and sugar in a bowl with an electric mixer until creamy, then add in the egg and continue mixing until it's light and fluffy. Add the flour, lemon juice and zest, baking powder and salt and combine until you end up with a ball of dough. Cover and place in the fridge for around 2 hours to firm up.

Preheat your oven to 180°C/350°F/gas 4. Flour your work surface and roll out the dough until it's around ½cm thick. Cut out shapes and place on to a baking tray lined with greaseproof paper. Sprinkle the biscuits with demerara sugar and bake for 10 to 12 minutes until the biscuits are lightly golden and light brown at the edges. Transfer to a wire rack to cool, then tuck in!

# BEAUTIFUL BLACK FOREST CUPCAKES

## MAKES 12 CUPCAKES

These mouth-watering cupcakes are my take on that great old-fashioned cake – Black Forest gâteau. I've made them in muffin cases this time so that there's plenty of room for all the gorgeous filling. Just make sure you whisk the eggs really well so that your cakes come out all lovely and light.

250g good-quality dark chocolate
(70% cocoa solids), broken into pieces
150g unsalted butter, cut into cubes
6 large eggs, preferably free-range
or organic
175g caster sugar
75g ground almonds

2 tablespoons plain flour
200ml double cream
1 vanilla pod, halved lengthways
and seeds scraped out,
pod reserved
zest and juice of 1 orange
250g frozen Black Forest fruits

Preheat your oven to 180°C/350°F/gas 4. Line a muffin tray with 12 paper cases. Pop the chocolate in a heatproof bowl and place over a pan of simmering water until melted, making sure the bowl and water don't touch. Add the butter, mix thoroughly, then put to one side.

Whisk the eggs until pale and thick, then stir in 125g of the caster sugar, the ground almonds and flour. Gently fold in the melted chocolate. Divide the mixture between the 12 cases then bake for 16 to 20 minutes until cooked through but still springy to the touch. You can check if your cakes are done by sticking a cocktail stick into the centre of one of them. If it comes out clean they're cooked. Don't worry if the cocktail stick is slightly moist, the egg will continue cooking as the cakes cool. Transfer to a wire rack and leave to cool.

Whip the cream and vanilla seeds in a bowl until you get soft peaks. Set aside.

Heat the orange zest and juice, vanilla pod and remaining sugar in a pan until the sugar has dissolved completely. Add the frozen fruits and cook for 8 to 10 minutes until soft. Allow to cool, then strain through a sieve, reserving the syrup. Return the syrup to the pan and reduce over a medium heat until thick.

Using a teaspoon, scoop out a 10p-sized hole from each cake's centre to just under halfway down. Fill with a heaped teaspoon of fruit. Top with cream and a drizzle of syrup.

# BUTTERNUT SQUASH MUFFINS WITH A FROSTY TOP

## MAKES 16 MUFFINS OR 36 CUPCAKES

The skin of a butternut squash goes deliciously chewy and soft when cooked, so there's no need to peel it off. Give these little cakes a go – they're a perfect naughty-but-nice treat.

400g butternut squash, skin on, deseeded and roughly chopped
350g light soft brown sugar
4 large eggs, preferably free-range or organic
a pinch of sea salt
300g plain flour, unsifted
2 heaped teaspoons baking powder
a handful of walnuts
1 teaspoon ground cinnamon
175ml olive oil

**for the frosted cream topping**
zest of 1 clementine
zest of 1 lemon and juice of ½ a lemon
140ml soured cream
2 heaped tablespoons icing sugar, sifted

**optional:** lavender flowers or rose petals
1 vanilla pod, halved lengthways and seeds scraped out
100g icing sugar

Preheat your oven to 180°C/350°F/gas 4. Line your muffin or cake tray with paper cases. Whizz the squash in a food processor until finely chopped. Add the sugar, and crack in the eggs. Add a pinch of salt, the flour, baking powder, walnuts, cinnamon and olive oil and whizz together until well beaten. You may need to pause the machine at some point to scrape the mixture down the sides with a rubber spatula. Try not to overdo it with the mixing – you want to just combine everything and no more.

Fill the paper cases three-quarters of the way up with the cake mixture. Bake in the preheated oven for 20 to 25 minutes if making muffins and for 10 to 12 minutes for cupcakes. Check to see whether they are cooked properly by sticking a wooden skewer or a knife right into one of the cakes – if it comes out clean, they're done. If it's a bit sticky, pop them back into the oven for a little longer. Remove from the oven and leave the cakes to cool on a wire rack.

As soon as they're in the oven, make your runny frosted topping. Place most of the clementine zest, all the lemon zest and the lemon juice in a bowl. Add the soured cream, icing sugar and vanilla seeds and mix well. Taste and have a think about it – adjust the amount of lemon juice or icing sugar to balance the sweet and sour. Put into the fridge until your cakes have cooled down and you're ready to serve, then spoon the topping on to the cakes as and when you want to eat them.

Serve on a lovely plate (or on a cake stand if you're feeling elegant, or on a rustic slab if you're more of a hunter-gatherer type!), with the rest of the clementine zest sprinkled over. For an interesting flavour and look, a few dried lavender flowers or rose petals are fantastic.

# SEA SALT AND CARAMEL CHOCOLATE CAKE SERVES 8 TO 10

Salted caramel might sound mad but it works! The creamy filling and dense chocolate sponge are magic, and the crunchy peanut brittle tops things off nicely. You only need a little brittle for the cake, so snap up and sell the rest. If you can't get hold of unsalted peanuts you can always wash some salted ones – just make sure you dry them off properly.

225g butter, at room temperature, plus extra for greasing
225g caster sugar
3 tablespoons cocoa powder, plus extra for dusting
4 large eggs, preferably free-range or organic
200g self-raising flour, sifted
1 teaspoon baking powder
200g caramel sauce

1 teaspoon sea salt
200ml double cream
1 vanilla pod, halved lengthways and seeds scraped out
300ml double cream

**for the peanut brittle**
450g caster sugar
200g unsalted peanuts
a knob of butter, for greasing

Preheat your oven to 180°C/350°F/gas 4. Grease and line a 20cm spring form cake tin. In a clean bowl beat the butter and sugar until light and fluffy. Add the cocoa, eggs, flour and baking powder and mix well.

Spoon the mixture into the prepared cake tin and bake in the hot oven for 40 to 45 minutes. Check on it after 40 minutes, and insert a skewer into the centre of the cake – if it comes out clean, it's done. Remove from the oven and leave to cool in the tin for 10 minutes, then carefully turn out on to a wire rack to cool completely.

Meanwhile, make the brittle. Put the sugar and 200ml water into a pan on a medium heat for about 10 minutes until the sugar has dissolved. Turn the heat up and after 10 to 15 minutes the sugar will begin to caramelize. Add your peanuts. Don't touch or taste the caramel, as it can burn badly, and don't be tempted to stir the mixture – just gently swirl the pan every now and then. When it turns a beautiful caramel colour, pour on to a greased non-stick tray and use a palette knife to push it out to about ½cm thick. Allow to cool for 15 minutes, then bash it up as you like.

Once the cake is cool, run a long knife around the middle, scoring and turning as you go, until the two lines join up. Carefully turn and cut into your cake, going deeper each time until you end up with two round halves.

To make your filling, mix the caramel with the sea salt then spread over the cut side of the bottom half of your cake. Whisk the cream with the vanilla seeds until it forms soft peaks, then spoon on top of the salted caramel. Carefully place the top half of the cake on top then dust with cocoa powder and the crushed peanut brittle.

# CARROT AND HONEY CAKE

SERVES 12

If you've never made a carrot cake before, give this recipe a try and I bet you'll be surprised by how easy it is to make, and how quickly everyone devours their slice.

285g butter, softened, plus extra
  for greasing
200g light soft brown sugar
3 tablespoons runny honey
5 eggs, preferably free-range
  or organic, separated
juice and zest of 1 orange
170g self-raising flour, sifted
1 slightly heaped teaspoon
  baking powder
1 x 100g pack ground almonds
1 x 100g pack walnuts, chopped

1 heaped teaspoon ground cinnamon
a pinch of ground cloves
a pinch of ground nutmeg
1–2 balls stem ginger, finely chopped
285g carrots, peeled and grated
a pinch of sea salt

**for the icing**
½ x 250g pot mascarpone cheese
½ x 300ml pot soured cream
85g icing sugar
juice and zest of 2 limes

Preheat your oven to 180°C/350°F/gas 4. Grease a 20cm square tin and line it with greaseproof paper.

Beat the butter and sugar together by hand in a large bowl, or in a food processor, until pale and fluffy. Beat in the honey, then the egg yolks, one by one, and add the orange juice and zest. Stir in the flour and baking powder, then add the ground almonds, walnuts, cinnamon, cloves, nutmeg, ginger and finally the grated carrots.

Whisk the egg whites with a pinch of salt until stiff, then fold them into the cake mixture. Scoop into the cake tin and cook for about 50 minutes until risen and golden. To test if it's cooked, insert a skewer into the centre – it should come out clean. Allow to cool in the tin for 10 minutes, then turn out on to a wire rack and leave for at least 1 hour to cool.

Meanwhile, make your icing. Mix the mascarpone, soured cream, icing sugar and lime juice together in a bowl. Fold through most of the lime zest, then spread over the top of the cake. Sprinkle over the remaining lime zest to decorate.

# BLUEBERRY BAKEWELL TART

SERVES 8

There's nothing more rewarding than baking a tart yourself, and this one never fails to impress. Rather than go down the traditional route, I've used blueberry jam in the base then topped the tart with lemon icing, which cuts through the sweetness of the almond filling beautifully.

2 heaped tablespoons plain flour, plus extra for dusting
375g sweet shortcrust pastry
200g butter, at room temperature
200g golden caster sugar
3 large eggs, preferably free-range or organic
1 vanilla pod, halved lengthways and seeds scraped out

200g ground almonds
5 heaped tablespoons blueberry jam
25g flaked almonds
zest and juice of 1 lemon
4 heaped tablespoons icing sugar
crème fraîche, to serve

Preheat your oven to 180°C/350°F/gas 4. Dust a clean work surface and a rolling pin with flour. Roll out the pastry until it's ½cm thick, then roll it up around your rolling pin, and unroll it over a clean 25cm loose-bottomed tart tin. Ease the pastry into the tin, gently pressing it into the corners. Trim off any excess then prick the pastry all over with a fork and place in the freezer for 30 minutes to firm up.

Meanwhile, whizz the butter and the sugar in a food processor until smooth. With the processor still running, crack in the eggs, one by one, followed by the vanilla seeds, flour and ground almonds and, as soon as the mixture comes together, turn off.

Place the tart tin on a baking tray. Scrunch up a large square of greaseproof paper, then flatten it out and use it to loosely line the pastry case. Fill it with uncooked rice or dried beans and bake for about 10 minutes, or until just golden at the edges (this is called baking blind). Carefully remove the rice or beans and paper (keep the rice or beans to use another time), then bake for a further 5 to 7 minutes, or until golden all over. Spoon in the jam and spread it out to the edges. Add the almond butter mix over the top, sprinkle with the flaked almonds and return to the oven to cook for 30 minutes until golden. Remove from the oven and leave to cool.

Finely grate the zest of the lemon, and mix with the icing sugar. Squeeze in just enough lemon juice to make a thick, runny paste, and drizzle this all over the cooled tart. Cut into wedges and serve with dollops of crème fraîche.

# STICKY TOFFEE CUPCAKES
## MAKES ABOUT 12 CUPCAKES

I used to love cupcakes as a kid and, while mucking about with a sticky-toffee-pudding recipe, I came up with these little beauties – they always put a smile on my face.

30g sultanas
30g dried apricots
30g dates
1 teaspoon baking powder
140g self-raising flour
30g dark muscovado sugar
1 tablespoon golden syrup
1 large egg, preferably free-range
  or organic
30g butter, melted

**for the chocolate topping**
40g butter
40g caster sugar
40g good-quality dark chocolate
(70% cocoa solids)
70ml double cream

Preheat your oven to 200°C/400°F/gas 6. In a food processor, blitz the sultanas, apricots, dates, baking powder and a little of the flour (just enough to stop the fruit sticking to the blades). If you don't have a food processor, you can chop everything very finely by hand.

Put this mixture into a bowl with the muscovado sugar, golden syrup, egg and the melted butter and stir together. Add 140ml very hot water and the remaining flour and mix well with a whisk. Divide the mixture between 12 cupcake cases (I like to double up the cases to give the mixture a bit more hold) and place on a baking tray. Bake in the preheated oven for about 15 minutes. You can check to see if the cakes are cooked by sticking a cocktail stick into the middle of one of them. Remove it after 5 seconds and if it comes out clean they're cooked; if slightly sticky they'll need a bit longer, so put them back in the oven for a few minutes until golden and cooked through. Remove the cakes from the oven and let them cool on a rack.

Meanwhile, melt all the chocolate-topping ingredients in a saucepan and let it bubble for a while until darkened in colour slightly. Try not to stir it too much. Remove from the heat and let the sauce cool until it thickens. When your cakes have cooled add a blob of the topping to each cupcake.

# CHILDREN'S PARTY CAKE

SERVES 12

Everyone needs a reliable party cake, and this is mine. It looks the business, is delicious served with cream and even has some fresh fruit in it. It'll keep for a day, so you can make it ahead of time if you like. What more can I say? Just tuck in!

200g butter, at room temperature, plus extra for greasing
4 tablespoons cocoa powder
3 large oranges
200g caster sugar
3 large eggs, preferably free-range or organic
200g self-raising flour

1 teaspoon baking powder
200ml double cream

**for the chocolate topping**
50g butter
50g good-quality dark chocolate (70% cocoa solids), broken up
50g icing sugar

Preheat your oven to 180°C/350°F/gas 4. Line the bases of two 20cm cake tins with greaseproof paper, then grease the sides of the tin with a little of the butter.

Add 60ml of boiling water to the cocoa powder and mix until smooth. Grate the zest of 2 oranges and put to one side. In another bowl, beat the sugar and butter until fluffy. Gradually add the cocoa mixture, eggs, flour, baking powder and the orange zest, and mix well.

Divide the mixture between the cake tins and bake in the oven for 20 to 25 minutes. To check the cakes are cooked, stick a skewer into the middle and leave it for 5 seconds. If it comes out clean, the cake is ready. Allow them to cool for 10 minutes, then remove from the tins and place on a cooling rack.

Meanwhile, place the butter and chocolate in a heatproof bowl, sift in the icing sugar then place over a pan of lightly simmering water. Make sure the water isn't boiling and the bottom of the bowl doesn't touch the water, or you will burn the chocolate. Zest the remaining orange, putting the zest to one side, then cut the orange in half and squeeze 3 tablespoons of juice into the bowl. Stir until melted and fully combined, then allow to cool. Whip the double cream until you have soft peaks. Segment the two other zested oranges with a small, sharp knife and quickly pat dry with kitchen paper.

Remove the greaseproof paper from the sponges and place one on a plate or cake stand. Spread over the cream and arrange the orange segments on top. Sandwich the second sponge on top and press down slightly. Drizzle the chocolate topping over the cake and leave to firm slightly. Sprinkle over the remaining orange zest to decorate.

# CHOCOLATE BROWNIES

MAKES 12 BROWNIES

One of these is never enough. They are nutty, chocolaty and delicious and people will go mad for them, so you should make loads! If you're not a fan of walnuts, try the recipe with dried cherries, apricots or pecan nuts – they're just as good.

125g unsalted butter, plus extra for greasing
100g good-quality dark chocolate (70% cocoa solids), broken into small pieces
4 large eggs, preferably free-range or organic

300g caster sugar
100g self-raising flour
a small pinch of sea salt
125g shelled walnuts
icing sugar, for dusting

Preheat your oven to 190°C/375°F/gas 5. Grease a 17cm x 25cm baking tin with a little butter, then cut a square of greaseproof paper to fit neatly in the bottom.

Melt the chocolate and butter in a glass bowl over a pan of simmering water, making sure the bowl doesn't touch the water, then remove from the heat and set aside.

Mix the eggs, sugar, flour and salt together in a bowl and when combined add in the melted chocolate and butter mixture. Sprinkle in the walnuts, then stir and fold together, being careful not to over-mix.

Spread the mixture evenly into the prepared cake tin and bake on the middle shelf of the oven for 16 to 19 minutes, or until a crust has formed. They should still be a bit wobbly (you don't want them to be really cooked through like a cake).

Allow the brownies to cool slightly then cut into chunky squares. Serve with a dusting of icing sugar over the top. Delicious!

# STICKY RHUBARB AND GINGER CAKE

## SERVES 8 TO 10

You can get hold of rhubarb for most of the year, but the forced stuff is so wonderfully pink and flavoursome that I just had to show it off on the top of this stunning cake. It's wonderful and moist, so it will keep well for a few days.

200g butter, plus extra for greasing
flour, for dusting
250g rhubarb
100g caster sugar
2 tablespoons stem ginger syrup
150g dark brown sugar
2 tablespoons golden syrup

150ml full-fat milk
2 large eggs, preferably free-range or organic
300g self-raising flour
2 teaspoons ground ginger
3–4 balls stem ginger, finely chopped and 2 tablespoons of the syrup

Preheat your oven to 180°C/350°C/gas 4. Line the base of a 20cm round cake tin with greaseproof paper, then butter and dust the sides with flour.

Slice the rhubarb into 4cm lengths and place in a pan with the caster sugar, 3 tablespoons of water and the stem ginger syrup. Bring to the boil then poach over a low heat for 5 minutes until the rhubarb is soft but still holding its shape.

Meanwhile, melt the butter, brown sugar and golden syrup in a pan over a low heat. Once melted and combined, set aside to cool. Whisk the milk and eggs together then add the cooled butter mixture and stir in the flour and the ground and chopped ginger.

Pour the cake mix into the prepared tin. Carefully arrange the rhubarb on top of the mixture, reserving the remaining syrup for later. Bake in the middle of the oven for 1 hour and 20 minutes until risen and golden. If it looks as if it might catch, cover the top of the cake with tin foil for the last 15 minutes of cooking. To check it's cooked, insert a skewer into the centre of the cake – if it comes out clean, you'll know it's done.

Remove from the oven, spoon over the reserved rhubarb syrup and leave to cool completely in the tin before serving. Delicious with a dollop of crème fraîche or a helping of custard.

# HOME-MADE FUDGE

MAKES 35 TO 40 PIECES

Good home-made fudge makes a wicked treat. These little cubes pack such an intense hit of sugar that it doesn't take many to satisfy a sweet tooth. Fudge needs a lot of love and attention while it's cooking so make sure you've got enough time to make it without any distractions. The other thing I will say is that you need to be sensible when cooking with hot sugar and make sure you don't muck about or take your eye off the pan. Once the fudge has cooled, you can either sell it at your bake sale one cube at a time, or pop a few cubes in some clear bags and tie them with ribbon to make them look pretty.

125g butter, plus extra
  for greasing
1 x 410g tin evaporated milk
3 tablespoons double cream

500g caster sugar
250g light soft brown sugar

Get yourself a small bowl of cold water ready. Grease a 20cm square cake tin with butter and put aside. Put the milk, cream and butter in a large, heavy-bottomed saucepan. Bring to boil on a high heat, stirring until the butter has melted and everything is combined.

Take the pan off the heat and add the sugar. Stir until the sugar has dissolved and the mixture is smooth. Place the pan back over a medium heat and bring to the boil, stirring constantly – this will take about 5 to 10 minutes. When it's at a rapid boil, reduce the heat to low, but you want the mixture to remain foamy and still be bubbling away. Cook and stir for a further 20 to 30 minutes, or until the mixture turns from golden to light brown, and when you drop a little into the bowl of cold water it forms a soft squidgy ball. At this point, take the pan off the heat and beat with a wooden spoon for 5 to 10 minutes until thick and fudgey.

Pour the fudge mixture into your prepared tin and leave to cool until firm, then tip out on to a board and cut into squares.

# THANKS TO...

...ALL THE LOVELY PEOPLE THAT HELPED ME PUT THIS LITTLE BOOK TOGETHER. BIG LOVE TO THE PENGUIN GANG: TOM WELDON, JOHN HAMILTON, LINDSEY EVANS, LAURA HERRING, SARAH FRASER, JULIETTE BUTLER AND NICK LOWNDES. THANKS TO PAUL BLOW FOR DONATING HIS WICKED ILLUSTRATING SKILLS. SHOUT OUT TO THE COMIC RELIEF TEAM: LOUISE WICKSTEAD, ANNE-CECILE BERTHIER, KEVIN CAHILL, RICK SCOTT AND HELENA JENNISON. LOVE TO DAVID LOFTUS FOR HIS BRILLIANT PHOTOGRAPHY, AND ALSO TO DAN JONES FOR THE IMAGE ON PAGE 13. THANKS TO MY TEAM: KATIE BOSHER, BETHAN O'CONNOR AND REBECCA WALKER ON WORDS, AND JODENE JORDAN AND PHILLIPPA SPENCE FOR THEIR HELP WITH RECIPE TESTING. TO THE PRINTER GRAPHICOM FOR HELPING OUT MASSIVELY WITH THE PRODUCTION COSTS AND TO ALTAIMAGE FOR DONATING THE COLOUR REPRODUCTION WE COULDN'T DO THIS WITHOUT YOUR HELP.

Penguin Books Ltd, 80 Strand, London WC2R 0RL, England

www.penguin.com

This edition copyright © Jamie Oliver, 2011

Cover and reportage photography © David Loftus, 2010

Illustrations © Paul Blow, 2011, paulblow/eastwing.co.uk

Food photography © David Loftus, 2001, 2005, 2006, 2007, 2009, 2010 except on page 13
Beautiful Black Forest Cupcakes © Dan Jones, 2009

Some of the recipes in this book were taken from Jamie's books: *Jamie at Home*, *Jamie's America* and *Happy Days with the Naked Chef*, all published by Michael Joseph/Penguin

Printed in Italy by Graphicom

ISBN: 978-0-241-95425-6

Comic Relief, registered charity 326568 (England/Wales); SC039730 (Scotland)